BUILT FOR SUCCESS

THE STORY OF

Wal-Mart

CREATIVE
PAPER BACKS

Published by Creative Paperbacks
P.O. Box 227, Mankato, Minnesota 56002
Creative Paperbacks is an imprint of The Creative Company
www.thecreativecompany.us

DESIGN BY **ZENO DESIGN**
PRODUCTION BY **CHRISTINE VANDERBEEK**
ART DIRECTION BY **RITA MARSHALL**

Printed by Corporate Graphics in the United States of America

PHOTOGRAPHS BY Alamy (Marc F. Henning, Jeremy Hogan,
Kristoffer Tripplaar, Jim West), AP Images (J. Scott Applewhite),
Getty Images (Michael L. Abramson/Time & Life Pictures,
Daniel Acker/Bloomberg, American Stock, Bradley C. Bower/
Bloomberg, China Photos, Thomas Cooper, Mike Fuentes/
Bloomberg, Beth Hall/Bloomberg, Chris Hondros, John Mcgrail/
Time & Life Pictures, Gilles Mingasson, Scott Olson, Diana
Walker/Time & Life Pictures)

Copyright © 2012 Creative Paperbacks
International copyright reserved in all countries. No part of
this book may be reproduced in any form without written
permission from the publisher.

Wal-Mart® and the products discussed in this book are either
trademarks or registered trademarks of Wal-Mart Stores, Inc.
Trademarks associated with products of other companies
mentioned are the trademarks of their respective owners. This
is not an official publication of Wal-Mart Stores, Inc., and the
views set out herein are solely those of the author.

**THE LIBRARY OF CONGRESS HAS CATALOGED THE HARDCOVER
EDITION AS FOLLOWS:**

Gilbert, Sara.
The story of Wal-Mart / by Sara Gilbert.
p. cm. — (Built for success)
Includes bibliographical references and index.
Summary: A look at the origins, leaders, growth, and operations of Wal-Mart, the discount retailing company whose first
store opened in 1962 and which today is one of the largest
corporations in the world.
ISBN 978-1-60818-064-6 (hardcover)
ISBN 978-0-89812-662-4 (pbk)
1. Wal-Mart (Firm)—History—Juvenile literature. 2. Discount
houses (Retail trade)—United States—History—Juvenile
literature. 3. Walton, Sam, 1918–1992. I. Title. II. Series.

HF5429.215.U6G55 2011
381'.1490973—dc22   2010031370

CPSIA: 110310 P01382

First edition

9 8 7 6 5 4 3 2 1

BUILT FOR SUCCESS

THE STORY OF

Wal-Mart

SARA GILBERT

As Sam Walton prepared to open a new store in Rogers, Arkansas, in the summer of 1962, he ran a series of ads in the local newspaper promoting the deals shoppers would find at the new retail outlet: a Sunbeam coffeemaker, usually priced at $19.95, for just $13.47; a $100 Polaroid camera for $74.37, and a lawnmower discounted from $59.95 to $37.77. The ads worked. When the store celebrated its grand opening on July 2, 1962, thousands of people showed up. They crowded into the 18,000-square-foot (1,672 sq m) store and found the entire space filled with tables laden with merchandise—clothing, toys, sporting goods, shampoos, small appliances, shoes, housewares, and more. Then they lined up at the three checkout stands and made the first Wal-Mart purchases in history.

CHAPTER ONE

A Store Is Born

When 22-year-old Sam Walton graduated from the University of Missouri in 1940, he began working as a management trainee at a J.C. Penney store in Des Moines, Iowa. He loved waiting on customers, and his personable nature made it easy for him to sell them clothing and other household items.

By the time he left that store in 1942, he had decided that he would be a retailer for the rest of his life—although he had to spend a few years in the United States Army first. When his time was up, he told his new bride, Helen, that he wanted to run his own retail store.

Helen Walton's only request was that they set up shop in a small town—one whose population did not exceed 10,000. So Walton's first operation, which opened in 1945, was a Ben Franklin **franchise** in the town of Newport, Arkansas, which had a population of 7,000. Walton's store sold everything from clothing to ice cream cones and became the best-selling Ben Franklin in the state. Then, in 1950, he moved Helen and their four children to the even smaller town of Bentonville, Arkansas (population 3,000), and purchased an established variety store there. He renamed it Walton's Five and Dime. By 1960, he had opened 15 Walton's Five and Dimes in Arkansas, Missouri, and Kansas.

Sam Walton became an Eagle Scout as a teenager and a captain in the U.S. Army during World War II

Even then, however, Walton wasn't satisfied. He was convinced that discounting—buying huge quantities of products at reduced rates and selling them for low prices—was going to be the retail model of the future, and he was determined to open his own discount store. He talked his brother Bud into putting up a couple thousand dollars, and the manager of one of his stores added another thousand or so. Walton and his wife went to the bank to borrow much of the remaining $350,000 they needed to open their first discount store.

Walton decided to build his first store in Rogers, Arkansas, a slightly larger town just a few miles away from Bentonville. It opened in 1962—the same year that Kmart, Woolco, and Target were launched in other parts of the country. Walton named his store Wal-Mart at the suggestion of a manager and hung two additional phrases on the front of the building: "We Sell for Less" and "Satisfaction Guaranteed."

Walton was certainly satisfied by that store's performance. Sales at the Rogers Wal-Mart, where about 25 employees were paid between 50 and 60 cents an hour to stack everything from automotive supplies to sporting goods on tables, totaled almost $1 million in the store's first year. That was far better than the $200,000 that the strongest of his variety stores had brought in. But Walton realized he could make even more money if he had more stores. So in 1964, he opened a 12,000-square-foot (1,115 sq m) barn-like building in nearby Harrison and a 35,000-square-foot (3,252 sq m) outlet in the larger town of Springdale. Almost immediately, the Springdale Wal-Mart sold better than the other two, thanks to the town's larger population. "I knew we were on to something," Walton said. "I knew in my bones it was going to work."

Following his convictions, Walton opened another store in 1965, two more in both 1966 and 1967, and five more in both 1968 and 1969, all in rural Arkansas, Oklahoma, and Missouri. At the time, Walton was primarily leasing existing buildings, including an abandoned Coca-Cola bottling plant. "Our stores didn't really look good," he admitted. "They weren't professional at all." But customers

Sam Walton's first store, in Bentonville, Arkansas, is today a visitor's center called Birthplace of Wal-Mart

weren't coming because of the buildings. They were looking for deals. And offering deals was what Walton did best.

Walton scouted out the best prices he could get from distributors, ordered the products in bulk, and then set a standard **markup** for 30 percent of the price he paid for an item—which meant that he could sell products for much less than his competitors, who had to pay more because they weren't buying in such large quantities. Sometimes, he'd forgo a markup of any kind just to get customers into his stores, where he hoped they would find other items to buy as well. When the Springdale store opened, he lured customers in by advertising tubes of toothpaste for 27 cents apiece.

By the end of 1969, Walton had opened 18 Wal-Mart stores, and he visited each location regularly. He always carried a yellow notepad with him so he could jot down which items were selling well and which weren't. He also toured competing stores. In 1964, he went to a Kmart near Chicago and found a clerk he could pepper with questions. Don Soderquist, a future Wal-Mart executive who was working for a competitor at the time, was shopping at the same Kmart and heard Walton asking the clerk about how often Kmart ordered, how much was ordered, and how **inventory** was tracked. Soderquist, who recognized Walton, asked him what he was doing. "Oh, this is just part of the educational process," Walton replied.

In 1969, Walton's Wal-Mart stores brought in combined sales of approximately $9 million. Although that didn't come close to the $800 million that the 250 Kmart stores were collectively bringing in, Walton was sure his strategy for success was working. And he was determined to keep the momentum going.

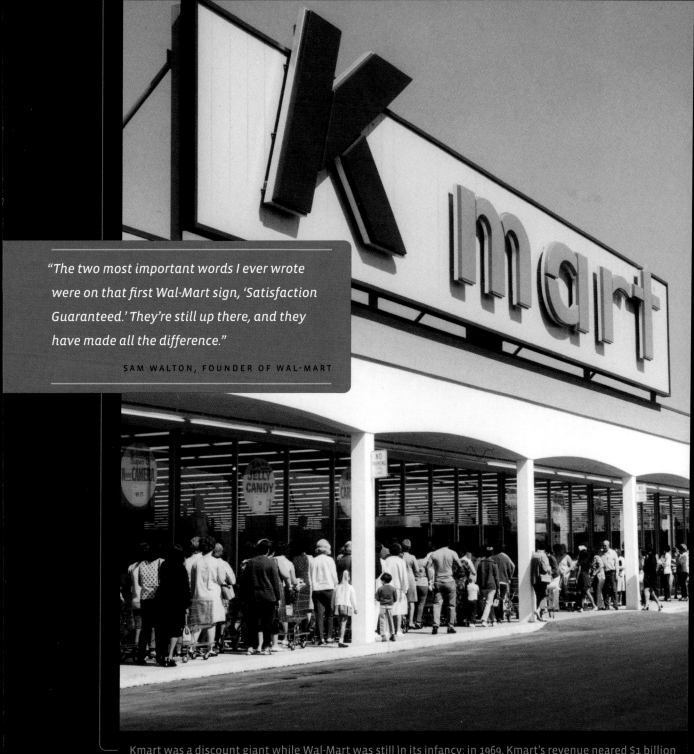

> *"The two most important words I ever wrote were on that first Wal-Mart sign, 'Satisfaction Guaranteed.' They're still up there, and they have made all the difference."*
>
> SAM WALTON, FOUNDER OF WAL-MART

Kmart was a discount giant while Wal-Mart was still in its infancy; in 1969, Kmart's revenue neared $1 billion

Sam Walton's original Bentonville office

GROWING UP WALTON

Sam Walton was born during the Great Depression—a time when many Americans had barely enough money for necessities such as food, let alone any extras. He watched his father work long hours as a farmer, a banker, and a real-estate agent to support his family. Even as a young- ster, Walton worked hard to help earn money. He delivered milk to neighbors after school, ran several paper routes, sold magazine sub- scriptions, and raised and sold rab- bits and pigeons. But he didn't use the money he made to buy toys or other luxuries for himself. Instead, his parents taught him to save—a lesson that followed him all his life. Even when he became a billionaire later in life, Walton was still frugal. "We don't need to buy a yacht," he wrote in his autobiography, *Made in America*. "We just don't have those kinds of needs and ambitions."

CHAPTER TWO

Going Gangbusters

Walton spent most of 1970 preparing for the growth that he was anticipating in the next decade. The first order of business was to open Wal-Mart's expansive new headquarters on a 12.5-acre (5 ha) plot of land outside Bentonville.

The plans included office space for the company's growing **executive** team—made up of men whom Walton had strategically recruited to help oversee operations— as well as a 60,000-square-foot (5,574 sq m) distribution center. The center housed large quantities of products that were ordered from suppliers and then kept there until they were needed by the stores, which were all within a 250-mile (402 km) radius of Bentonville at the time. The Bentonville distribution center, which later became one of the first in the industry to use computers to track inventory, served as a model for future distribution centers, which were opened in different parts of the country as Wal-Mart grew, ensuring that stores' shelves could be restocked quickly.

But new stores, new buildings, and new employees (by 1970, Wal-Mart had 1,500 people on its **payroll**) all added to the operating expenses of the business. Walton had always been notoriously tight with his money and was beginning to get a little concerned about the loans he and Helen were taking out to finance the company's growth. By the time the new headquarters opened, the Waltons owed almost $2 million to different banks. "Helen and

Wal-Mart's early success was due in part to its innovative and efficient distribution centers

I were in debt up to our eyeballs," Walton admitted. "If everybody decided to call in their notes, we would be sunk."

That debt was one of the reasons that Walton decided in 1970 to take Wal-Mart public by offering **shares** of the company to investors. Not only did he need to start paying off some of his loans, but he also needed more cash on hand to keep expanding. He had already been forced to walk away from five towns where he wanted to build stores because of financial concerns. So on October 1, 1970, 300,000 shares of Wal-Mart **stock** were sold at $16.50 a share, bringing in a total of $4.6 million. Walton was thrilled—he could finally pay off much of his debt.

The funds raised by the **initial public offering** also allowed Walton to aggressively pursue new opportunities for expansion. In 1971, Wal-Mart stores opened in Kansas and Louisiana. Two years later, they were being built in Tennessee; franchises in Kentucky and Mississippi followed in 1974. By 1975, when the first Wal-Mart was built in Texas, the company boasted 125 stores with total sales of more than $340 million.

At that point, more than 7,500 "associates" were working in Wal-Mart stores. Walton, who prided himself on knowing something about everyone he worked with, could no longer keep up with whose kids were doing what. But he still wanted to maintain a familial atmosphere and a culture of cooperation at his stores. So he developed the Wal-Mart cheer, which he used at almost every meeting and whenever he visited a store: "Give me a W! Give me an A! Give me an L!," which continued until the name had been spelled out. "If I'm leading the cheer, you better believe we do it loud," Walton said.

Things were going so well for Wal-Mart that, in 1974, at the age of 56, Walton considered stepping back from the business. He was the chairman and chief executive officer (CEO), but he had hired a pair of executive vice presidents whom he thought he could entrust with more responsibility. One was Ferold Arend, who ran the **merchandising** side of the operation; the other was Ron Mayer,

The Wal-Mart cheer was born after Sam Walton witnessed a similar cheer in a Korean tennis ball factory

who was in charge of the company's finances and distribution.

Late in 1974, Walton promoted Mayer to CEO and chairman and made Arend president of the company. Walton became chairman of the executive committee and moved from his large office to a smaller space. His intention was to stay out of Mayer and Arend's way and let them make decisions, but that wasn't as easy as he had hoped. He continued to visit stores and hovered around the office. Mayer and Arend, meanwhile, openly disliked each other and frequently disagreed about company decisions—which made it harder for Walton to relinquish his role. "I failed at retirement worse than just about anything else I ever tried," he admitted later. "I just kept doing exactly the same thing I had been doing all the time."

The retirement experiment lasted for 30 months. One Saturday in June 1976, Walton called Mayer into his office. He explained that he wasn't ready to be retired and that he was returning as both CEO and chairman. Arend would remain as president, but Walton asked Mayer to accept the title of vice chairman and chief financial officer. Mayer chose instead to leave the company.

When Mayer left, several senior managers who had supported him left as well. The shuffling that followed put a dent in the company's stock prices. But it didn't stop people from shopping at Wal-Mart, which was operating 276 stores in 11 states by 1979. Combined, those stores brought in $1.2 billion in sales. Wal-Mart had become known, at least in the South, as a retail giant. But Walton had even bigger plans.

"...estion, Sam Walton is one of the ...e merchants. Period."

...MARCUS, COFOUNDER OF HOME DEPOT

Rollback
Smile, you're saving even more

Was $2 48

$2 3 8

The Wal-Mart name grew out of a conversation Sam Walton had with Bob Bogle, the manager of a Walton's Five and Dime in Bentonville, in the spring of 1962. Walton showed Bogle an index card with several names on it and asked which ones he liked best. All of the options were three or four words long—and Bogle thought that was too much. "I'd just keep the Walton name and make it a place to shop," he advised. Then he scribbled his own suggestion on the card: WALMART. He told his boss that it would save him money, because there were fewer letters to buy. A few days later, Bogle saw letters being hung at the new store. A *w*, an *a*, and an *l* were already up, and an *m* was going next. "You didn't have to be a genius to figure out what the name was going to be," Bogle said. "I just smiled and went on."

CHAPTER THREE

National Exposure

Wal-Mart had already grown big enough to pose a threat to competitors. In the late 1970s, Kmart had noticed Wal-Mart's growth, and even though the Michigan-based chain still had far more stores (more than 1,000) and much higher sales numbers than Wal-Mart, it decided to start moving into the small southern towns where Wal-Mart stores were already established.

Walton welcomed the challenge. He instructed his store managers to keep close track of the prices at Kmart and to not let the rival chain **undersell** Wal-Mart on anything. In Little Rock, that meant dropping the price of toothpaste to an unheard-of low price of six cents per tube. The strategy worked. "Once Kmart arrived, we worked even harder at pleasing our customers," Walton said. "They stayed loyal. This gave us a great surge of confidence in ourselves." So many people were shopping at Wal-Mart that in 1983 Walton began hiring "People Greeters" to stand at the entrance of all 551 stores and welcome shoppers into the building; Walton, who still flew around visiting his stores, occasionally took a shift as a People Greeter himself, offering a friendly welcome to his customers.

Wal-Mart's stock prices climbed to more than $81 a share in 1983, which was

Wal-Mart's customer service slogan appears on the trademark blue vests worn by all associates

great news for the company's many associates. Since 1971, every Wal-Mart employee—from vice president to store clerk—who worked at least 1,000 hours a year was eligible to participate in a **profit-sharing plan**. Wal-Mart contributed a percentage of its **profits** to each employee's plan, which was invested in Wal-Mart stock. As stock prices rose, the value of the profit-sharing plan did, too. It was a significant benefit for Wal-Mart's many hourly employees, who often earned minimum wage ($3.10 in 1980); through the course of their employment, many of these workers made more than $100,000 dollars from profit sharing.

Although Walton didn't often pay more than minimum wage to his hourly employees, he did want to reward them for the role they played in helping the company turn a profit. That's why he promised to dance the hula down Wall Street in New York City if Wal-Mart's profits in 1983 reached a new record. And that's why, on a chilly day in March 1984, the 65-year-old Walton buttoned a bright blue Hawaiian shirt over his suit coat, tied a grass skirt around his waist, and draped a pair of leis around his neck. Then he swiveled his hips, circled his arms and danced his way down the street. The stunt was shown on several newscasts that evening and made newspapers all around the country the next morning.

Walton avoided making profit-based promises after that. His company was growing exponentially, helped by the opening of the first Sam's Club location in Midwest City, Oklahoma, in 1983. Walton had visited a Price Mart in California earlier that year and decided to copy its business model. Sam's Clubs were open only to members, who paid an annual fee to shop at the warehouse-style store, where products were stacked from floor to ceiling in bulk packaging.

In 1988, the aging Walton decided to hand the title of CEO to David Glass, who had been president of Wal-Mart since 1984, but to remain involved in the company as chairman. At that time, more than 1,400 Wal-Marts and more than 100 Sam's Clubs were operating in 29 states. The company also introduced its first Supercenter that year, offering groceries in addition to the standard Wal-Mart

Sam Walton later admitted that his publicity-generating dance on Wall Street in 1984 "really embarrassed me"

fare of clothing, health and beauty products, toys, and household items. As the 1990s began, Wal-Mart opened its first international location in Mexico City.

But in the midst of all that good news came exceedingly bad news: Walton, who had battled leukemia in 1982, was diagnosed with multiple myeloma, a **malignant** cancer of the **bone marrow**, in 1989. The prognosis, doctors said, was bleak. Walton had an aggressive form of cancer for which there was no cure; standard treatments such as chemotherapy and radiation could push it into remission, but his doctors couldn't make any promises.

Walton sent a memo to his store managers, instructing them to share it with their associates, saying only that he had myeloma and that he was treating it with chemotherapy. "I feel so much better already," he wrote. "Hopefully within a month or two I'll begin my visitations over our Wal-Mart country."

Walton was back at work within months. He presided over the annual meeting in 1990, bouncing around the stage and boldly predicting that Wal-Mart would reach $130 billion in sales by the year 2000. But he also worked out of his home more often and began to skip regularly scheduled management meetings. By the end of 1991, Walton's cancer had progressed so far that he quit visiting stores.

In March 1992, Walton was wheeled into the auditorium at Wal-Mart headquarters in Bentonville to accept the Presidential Medal of Freedom—one of the country's highest civilian honors, which he was awarded for his **entrepreneurial** spirit—from president George H. W. Bush. He insisted on standing up when the president placed the medal around his neck and remained on his feet as the crowd of Wal-Mart employees packed into the room erupted in an emotional ovation that lasted several minutes. Days later, he was admitted to the hospital in Little Rock, and on April 5, 1992, at the age of 74, Sam Walton died.

"Clearly, Wal-Mart is more powerful than any retailer has ever been."

EDWARD FOX, HEAD OF SOUTHERN METHODIST
UNIVERSITY'S J.C. PENNEY CENTER
FOR RETAILING EXCELLENCE

Sam Walton passed away less than three weeks after being honored with the Medal of Freedom

Sam Walton and his family

In October 1985, *Forbes* magazine estimated Sam Walton's worth at $2.8 billion and labeled him "the richest man in America." Suddenly, he and his wife Helen were besieged by requests for interviews—and requests for money as well. Complete strangers would send letters detailing their needs, from new cars to dental work, asking for handouts. Producers from *The Lifestyles of the Rich and Famous* ambushed them on tennis courts, and reporters called their home at all hours. For a family unaccustomed to being in the spotlight, the attention was overwhelming and disconcerting. But despite the additional publicity, Sam still drove an old Chevy truck, with kennels for his bird dogs in the back, and he still got his hair cut at the barbershop in downtown Bentonville. Two years later, when the stock market crashed, and Wal-Mart stock dropped significantly, Walton was asked how it felt to lose half a billion dollars. "It's only paper," Walton replied.

CHAPTER FOUR

A Wal-Mart World

In 1990, Wal-Mart had surpassed Sears, Roebuck and Co. as the retailer with the most stores in the nation. But the company hadn't stopped looking for more opportunities to grow.

Glass fully intended to continue the aggressive pace of expansion that Walton had begun almost 30 years earlier. Glass was quiet and thoughtful, not quite as charming or charismatic as Walton, but he was an astute businessman. And he knew that the next frontier for Wal-Mart lay beyond America's borders.

Wal-Mart already had a presence in Mexico and Puerto Rico (where the company had opened a store in 1992), and in 1993, Glass began to operate Wal-Mart International from corporate headquarters in Bentonville. His goal was to extend Wal-Mart's retail model around the world, while fitting each store to the needs and customs of the country in which it was located by carrying appropriate products. A year later, the company bought 122 struggling Woolco stores in Canada and brought them back to life as Wal-Marts; it also opened 3 stores in Hong Kong. In 1995, it added locations in Argentina and Brazil (the latter where stores were known as Todo Dia, Portuguese for "All Day"). China followed in 1996.

Back at home, Wal-Mart had finally opened locations in all 50 states. In 1995, it found a site in Vermont, the last state without a Wal-Mart. Protesters had argued that the giant retailer would kill the independent businesses that served the state's

沃尔玛购物广场（上海南浦大

WAL★MART
SUPERCENTER

Wal-Mart opened a new store in Shanghai in July 2005, giving it 48 locations in all throughout China

quaint small towns, as had happened in some other locations where Wal-Mart had arrived. The protesters had the backing of the National Trust for Historic Preservation, which had declared Vermont's small towns (collectively) among the 11 most endangered historic places in the U.S. in 1993. To appease the activists, Wal-Mart decided not to construct a large building on the outskirts of town as it did in most cities, moving instead into a vacant Woolworth's store in a shopping center near downtown Bennington.

By the end of 1995, Wal-Mart was operating a total of 2,943 stores (including Wal-Marts, Sam's Clubs, and Supercenters) in 6 countries. Sales had increased dramatically under Glass's leadership. When he took over in 1988, the company was bringing in $20.6 billion in annual sales; by 1995, that figure had risen to $93.6 billion. By all accounts, he had capably filled the enormous shoes Walton had left behind.

Like Walton, Glass visited stores on a regular basis and occasionally took a shift as one of the People Greeters at the front doors of a Wal-Mart. Like Walton, he had a vision for steady growth. But Glass also had a greater understanding of how technology could transform the distribution of goods and had led the implementation of a computerized distribution system in 1978. Unlike Walton, who never appreciated computers, Glass saw computers and technology as key players in Wal-Mart's quest to cut administrative costs.

Glass's tenure was not without controversy—some of which was not entirely of his making. In the 1980s, Walton had prominently placed "Made in America" signs throughout his stores and had promoted buying American-made products. But in the early 1990s, reporters and other investigators started scrutinizing the labels of Wal-Mart's merchandise and found that many items, especially clothing, had been made in places such as China, India, and Bangladesh. Wal-Mart was even accused of working with suppliers who used child labor in **sweatshops**.

Sam's Club stores have a warehouse feel, as shoppers push big carts down wide aisles to buy bulk products

WAL·MART

Only after a television reporter confronted Glass on camera late in 1992 did he officially address that practice. In the spring of 1993, the company adopted certain standards for its **vendors**, mandating that workers be at least 15 years old and that they be paid a reasonable wage for their work. Although the standards were a start, some believed that the real test of Wal-Mart's commitment to fair labor practices would be in how those rules were enforced. "Setting standards is five percent of the work," said Simon Billenness, an analyst who helped Wal-Mart work through the process. "Ensuring compliance is 95 percent." Wal-Mart agreed to carry out assessments to make sure the rules were followed.

Labor relations were a global consideration for the company. By 1997, Wal-Mart had approximately 680,000 employees in the U.S., making it the country's largest private employer, and by the end of the decade, it had become the largest private employer in the world, with almost 1,140,000 associates worldwide. The company had managed to avoid **labor unions**, which would have demanded higher pay and better benefits, in its stores since 1962. Its profit-sharing plan had been designed to provide employees a benefit that unions couldn't offer. But as stock prices dipped in the early 1990s, making profit-sharing plans worth less, employees voiced their discontent.

In 1994, workers in four of the company's stores began trying to organize unions—and Wal-Mart officials fought back, sometimes by finding reasons to fire those workers. Over the next few years, more and more stores joined the unionization effort, each meeting the same defiance from management. But in 1997, the company lost its first battle; a store in Canada, where labor laws were more strict than in the U.S., successfully unionized. In the U.S., however, Wal-Mart had not allowed unions to form in any of its stores as of 2010.

"...w the effects that these superstores ...ey tend to suck the economic and ...e out of these downtowns, many of ...ther and die as a result."

...HARD MOE, PRESIDENT OF THE NATIONAL
TRUST FOR HISTORIC PRESERVATION

Union Yes! Wal-mart No!

David Glass

SWEATSHOP SCANDAL

When Wal-Mart CEO David Glass sat down to tape an interview for the *Dateline NBC* news show in December 1992, he had no idea what he was in for. When the reporter accused him of using sweatshops to produce Wal-Mart merchandise—with videotape of children in Bangladesh making Wal-Mart products as evidence—Glass was clearly uneasy. When shown a picture of a factory that had burned, killing 25 children, his only reply was, "There are tragic things that happen all over the world." He cut the interview short but two weeks later invited *Dateline* back. His staff had assured him that there were no children working at the factory that burned down, but when he announced this on camera, the reporter was clearly skeptical. The program, which depicted Wal-Mart in a negative light, aired on December 22, 1992. This time, Glass was prepared: He had coordinated a huge number of callers, who paralyzed the NBC switchboard with complaints about the story.

CHAPTER FIVE

Super Store

Wal-Mart started a new decade with a new leader: longtime Wal-Mart executive H. Lee Scott Jr. was named CEO when Glass announced his retirement late in 1999. In his first 5 years as CEO, Scott presided over the addition of more than 2,000 retail outlets and watched worldwide sales increase from $137 billion in 1999 to $312 billion in 2005.

Although he was not oblivious to complaints about Wal-Mart's low wages, **importation** policies, and other issues, such as environmental impact, Scott at first chose to follow the company's historical policy of remaining silent in the face of criticism. In 2005, however, he decided it was time to respond to what he said had become an **urban legend** about the company.

Scott announced the launch of a Web site, www.walmartfacts.com, that would provide "the unfiltered truth" about employee pay and benefits, as well as the company's **economic** and environmental impact on the towns it served throughout America and the world. "We've decided it's time to draw our own line in the sand," he said. "We want to set a tone that Wal-Mart Stores is going to be aggressive

Like Sam Walton, H. Lee Scott rose from humble beginnings in the South to become Wal-Mart's CEO

in taking care of customers and taking care of our associates."

The impact of Scott's new open-and-honest policy was helped by the company's response to Hurricane Katrina, which devastated the city of New Orleans and left a path of destruction throughout the Gulf Coast region in 2005. The company had hundreds of stores in the affected areas, including 126 that had to be closed because of the storm. Scott called a meeting of his top managers to discuss how the company could help. At that point, Wal-Mart had already promised $2 million in relief aid. "Should it be $10 million?" Scott asked.

Wal-Mart's contribution ended up being closer to $18 million in cash, as well as almost 100 truckloads of diapers, toothbrushes, and bottled water, and enough food to provide 100,000 meals. The company also promised a job to every worker displaced by the storm. Wal-Mart was lauded by former presidents Bill Clinton and George H. W. Bush, who joined forces to lead a fundraising campaign, and by officials in New Orleans.

The company's coordinated response helped quiet some of its harshest critics. So did the opening of two environmentally friendly stores in Texas and Colorado, both designed to save energy, conserve natural resources, and reduce pollution—all efforts made in response to complaints from activists who were critical of the size and wasteful use of resources at many Wal-Mart stores. The environmentally friendly stores, which tested both wind- and solar-generated power, were intended to be laboratories for technologies, materials, and landscaping ideas that could be integrated into other Wal-Mart buildings in the future. The company also began experimenting with reducing the packaging on its own line of products, which had been called excessive.

Despite the concerns voiced by many people, the 6,779 Wal-Mart stores in existence worldwide by 2006 remained quite busy. The company reported that an average of 176 million customers visited its stores each week that year. With record sales of $345 billion, the corporation had become not only the biggest retailer in the world but also the biggest company. In three months, it could

Wal-Mart's environmentally friendly Colorado store got some of its electricity from this huge wind turbine

sell more than what the second-largest retailer, Home Depot, could sell over the course of a full year.

Even in 2008, when an economic **recession** hurt revenues for most retailers, Wal-Mart sales remained strong, due in large part to its continued commitment to low prices on everyday products. In the third **quarter** of the year, the company posted a seven percent increase in sales.

As Wal-Mart weathered the economic storm, Scott decided late in 2008 that it was time to retire. In February 2009, Mike Duke, who had joined the company in 1995, was named Scott's successor. Duke moved into the wood-paneled office at Wal-Mart's headquarters that had previously belonged to just three other men: Scott, Glass, and Walton. As Duke settled in, he planned to continue the course of growth those three had already set for the company.

But while growth—especially internationally—was certainly part of Duke's plans for Wal-Mart's future, he had other items on his to-do list as well. Many of those revolved around the company's environmental impact. In the summer of 2009, he announced plans to create a rating system for all products sold in Wal-Mart stores. Ratings would be based on a range of environmental factors, from **emissions** to water use, and product labels would help consumers choose items that were more environmentally responsible. Early in 2010, he set goals to substantially reduce the company's **greenhouse gas** emissions and to become as energy efficient as possible. At the same time, Duke continued to explore opportunities to expand Wal-Mart's international reach into such countries as Russia.

Wal-Mart has always been open to new opportunities, from its humble beginnings as a discount store in the small town of Rogers, Arkansas, to its current stature as a retail giant with thousands of outlets around the world. Despite its amazing growth, Wal-Mart has maintained the vision that founder Sam Walton set for it in 1962: to provide the products people need at the lowest prices possible.

> "My big places to shop are Wal-Mart and Target—seriously. That is where half of my stuff comes from now."
>
> HOLLYWOOD ACTRESS KELLY PRESTON

Fresh Produce
Frutas y Verduras Frescas

Grocery
Víveres

Supercenter groceries accounted for 49 percent of Wal-Mart's sales in 2009 and 51 percent in 2010

WAL·MART

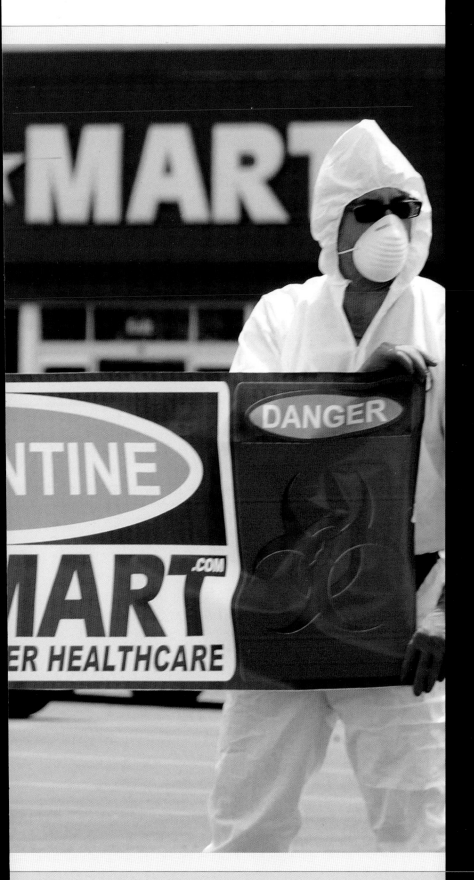

THE BOYCOTT BANDWAGON

In December 2005, Wal-Mart instructed all of its associates to wish store customers "Happy Holidays" instead of "Merry Christmas" in an effort to be accepting of all religious beliefs. That request set off one of the first nationwide boycotts of the retail giant, as some Christian groups who were offended that the company wouldn't recognize Christmas asked people not to shop there. Since then, dozens of other groups have also tried to boycott Wal-Mart stores, from various labor unions to gay-rights supporters protesting the company's refusal to offer insurance coverage for domestic partners. Even the Marijuana Policy Project initiated a boycott when an employee who legally used marijuana to treat cancer was fired for failing a drug test. The company occasionally responds to groups' concerns (the fired employee was given his job back, for example), but its sales figures have not been significantly affected by such protests.

GLOSSARY

bone marrow the tissue that fills bones and that produces red and white blood cells

economic having to do with the system of producing, distributing, and consuming goods within a society

emissions the waste discharged into the air by vehicle engines and other sources

entrepreneurial having the attitude or qualities of an entrepreneur, or a person who begins a new business

executive a decision-making leader of a company, such as the president or chief executive officer (CEO)

franchise a business authorized to sell a company's products or operate under its name

Great Depression a time from 1929 to 1939 when there was widespread unemployment in the U.S. and elsewhere in the world and a major decline in the production and sale of goods

greenhouse gas a gas, such as carbon dioxide, that is trapped in the atmosphere and has a warming effect on Earth

importation the act of buying goods from a foreign country, usually with the intention of selling them

initial public offering the first sale of stock by a company to the public; it is generally done to raise funds for the company, which is then owned by investors rather than by an individual or group of individuals

inventory the total of a company's merchandise that has not yet been sold

labor unions organizations of workers who join together to protect their common interest and to improve the conditions of their employment, including wages and hours

malignant something, such as a tumor or growth, that is dangerous to a person's health and often spreads throughout the body

markup an amount added to the price a store pays for an item to determine the cost customers will be charged

merchandising promoting the sale of products through advertising, sales, and displays

payroll a list of employees receiving wages or salaries, and the money each is paid

profits the amount of money that a business keeps after subtracting expenses from income

profit-sharing plan an arrangement in which an employer shares some of its profits with its employees, in the form of stocks, bonds, or cash

quarter one of four three-month intervals that together comprise the financial year; public companies must report certain data on a quarterly basis

recession a period of decline in the financial stability of a country or society that typically includes a drop in the stock market, an increase in unemployment, and a decline in home sales

shares the equal parts a company may be divided into; shareholders each hold a certain number of shares, or a percentage, of the company

stock shared ownership in a company by many people who buy shares, or portions, of stock, hoping the company will make a profit and the stock value will increase

sweatshops shops or factories in which employees work for long hours at low wages and under unhealthy conditions

undersell to sell a product or service at a lower price than a competitor

urban legend an often horrible or disturbing story or anecdote that is based on rumors and widely circulated as true, although usually it is not

vendors individuals or companies that supply products or services to another company

SELECTED BIBLIOGRAPHY

Barbaro, Michael, and Justin Gills. "Wal-Mart at Forefront of Hurricane Relief." *The Washington Post*, September 6, 2005. http://www.washingtonpost.com/wp-dyn/content/article/2005/09/05/AR2005090501598.html.

Donlon, J. P. "A Glass Act—Wal-Mart CEO David Glass, Chief Executive of the Year," *The Chief Executive*, July/August 1995.

Ortega, Bob. *In Sam We Trust: The Untold Story of Sam Walton, and How Wal-Mart Is Devouring America*. New York: Times Business, 2000.

Soderquist, Don. *The Wal-Mart Way: The Inside Story of the Success of the World's Largest Company*. Nashville, Tenn.: Thomas Nelson, 2005.

Vance, Sandra S., and Roy V. Scott. *Wal-Mart: A History of Sam Walton's Retail Phenomenon*. New York: Twayne Publishers, 1994.

Wal-Mart Stores. "History Timeline." Wal-Mart Corporate. http://walmartstores.com/aboutus.

Walton, Sam, with John Huey. *Made in America: My Story*. New York: Doubleday, 1992.

INDEX